Swimming With Dolphins

EVELYN MCKITTRICK

To Carolyn
From Evelyn
Enjoy!

Bright Pen

Visit us online at www.authorsonline.co.uk

A Bright Pen Book

First published in Great Britain 2014

Text Copyright © EVELYN McKITTRICK 2014
Cover Design Copyright © Tim Wander 2014
Photographs   © EVELYN McKITTRICK 2014

A CIP catalogue record for this book is available from the British Library.
ISBN 978-0-7552-1632-1

Authors OnLine Ltd.
19 The Cinques,
Gamlingay, Sandy,
Bedfordshire, SG19 3NU.
England.

This book is also available in e-book format, details of which are available at: www.authorsonline.co.uk .

*For David, Amanda
and Christopher.....
we are all still
swimming*

About the Book

It is never an easy task to group a collection of poems written over many years. Here you will find poems about family, poems about being old, poems which are thoughtful, or humorous, happy or sad. Some are philosophical, dealing with feelings about the world. There are those which are just fun. Some poems rhyme while others resist the temptation. Some poems refuse to slot into only one classification. They could comfortably be placed in a different group. Each reader will reach their own conclusions.

About the Author

Evelyn McKittrick was born and brought up in Belfast. After teaching there she moved to London to do a dance training.

Subsequently she has lived in several places in England, spent a year in Canada, before returning to England and then back to Northern Ireland. She now lives in Spain.

She has taught many poetry classes and worked for the WEA, also an organisation called WIP (Women into Politics) teaching women's studies.

On the way she gained a few degrees, B.A. Hons., M.Ed., M.A. Among her several interests, apart from writing poetry and plays, she is director of "The Littlest Theatre Company in the World" about which she is currently writing a book.

She occasionally reads tarot cards for her friends.

Acknowledgments

Any book is always a personal journey and a book of poetry perhaps more so. Some of these poems reach back over 20 years so I would like to thank David for continually chasing me to put the words onto paper.

Along any journey you always need help and it is often the people you meet who make the adventure special. So to all the people who have worked with me or influenced me over the years (and you know who you are) I say thank you. A special thanks to Anita Greg for her inspiring pictures.

To actually make this happen can I also thank Tim for his continual help, suggestions and recovery of my mixed up drafts, lost corrections and computerised mistakes. Judith, thanks to you as well.

Who would have thought that changing from paper and pen to keyboard and screen would be so confusing.

Swimming with Dolphins

EVELYN McKITTRICK

CONTENTS

POEMS INSPIRED BY ANITA'S PAINTINGS   47

PEOPLE AND PREDICAMENTS   65

THE OLD WOMAN   79

LOOKING IN AND LOOKING OUT 85

FOR FUN 99

CHILDHOOD

Never Having Swum With Dolphins She Is Afraid Of Other Poets

In the Tropic of Cancer
she watched a past life self-destruct,
and she, gutted, wholly consumed,
gobble, cluck, clack, - ululating
voices took a look inside her head.
Down the passage to where sea ebbed,
blood flowed, raw, wild.

The wild goat in Capricorn
scales the fish walls of never ending
brickbats in the belfry, hiding
the clanging, clanging of bad dreams,
forgotten dreams and the no dreams
of the wide – eyed life
where dreams are dead or dying.

She rang a garland conch shell
whose magic echoed far beyond a shore
from where a crabbed curve of shellfish
muttered a moonrise spell.
Returned to her clear message -song

sweet and bitter, murmuring of fins,
drowning, drowned ...
limits of perfect
isolation.

Trip To The Stars

A bright and happy moon
reminds me always
of an evening long past bedtime.
I hop skipped beside my father
and not to break the spell
I side-stepped every crack
under my moony feet.

"Look at the moons Daddy
Not up there in the sky,
down here in my shoes.
See all the small moons
blink at each other
in the black patent of
my Sunday shoes."

"Will Uncle Jack see that moon?"
My dad replied, "Not till morning."
For a moment I felt sorry
for Uncle Jack in America
and didn't feel jealous
of glamorous cousin Jean
gone to be a film star.
No moon till morning!

And happiness kept breaking out in me.
We were going to the pictures

just me and my father
and he would save me from
the big man in the high hat
who might sit in front
to hide my view of the moon
and the stars.

Reverie

Bedroom walls jig-saw-puzzled .
by new shadow shapes,
out-shadowing old street lamps.

Edges and corner pieces
of squat and ugly furniture
dissolve in the firelight,

into convex-concave curves.
Black magic wardrobe shadows
ebb and flow across the wallpaper rose pebbles,
caught and thrown, caught again.

In the dervish dance of the flames
pink roses blaze red, blacken and wither
as embers follow from flame,
turning the wall to fading sunset.

My father has made the fire
and I now must bear its heat.

Old mattress on old springs
finds out still tender places.
Familiar ever-changing lumps

of old socks, laddered nylons.

A home sewn party frock
buttons removed, together with
elastic torn from knickers,
disturb my slumbers.

Sunday shirt too frayed for workdays,
its much turned collar still turning
inside the patchwork of bleached flour bags.

Bits of this and that of different texture
and colour, drab to begin with,
are hidden away – makes no difference.

My mother has made the bed
and now I must lie in it.

Dead Of Night

I wake in the night
to hear rain falling
in the next room;
into the dark of my ear
my mother's weeping whisper,
"I must go, George,
she's slipping away".

Rustle of hasty dressing,
gentle screech of bedroom door
to wake my older sister –
the women of the house are gone
to attend to the dying
of their grandmother:
she is my grandmother too.

Alone in the dark
my twelve year old fears
all unknowing and nameless
prepare and prepare me...

"Daddy! Daddy!" the fear cries out,
"can I come into your bed?"
A silence I do not understand. Then,
"Wait till I get my trousers on".

The Weekly Visit

Armed to the teeth with her fine comb
Grannie performed the painful ritual,
forcing rebel locks to her order.
Her meticulous nit-picking voice
scraped through to the bone to the brain
as she began the interrogation.
Sorely I searched my head for a sin to tell,
something to confess, anything
to make her visit more interesting
and to shift the attention
from the hair washing and fine combing.

I hadn't kissed any boys
nor allowed any to kiss me.
Kissing was wrong
but the confessing of it
would have delighted Grannie,
"Men", she would say
with satisfaction, without explanation
"are only after one thing".

I could not admit to having got wrong
any spellings or tables,
to give Grannie a chance to say,
"Women need an education,
something to fall back on".

She made education sound like an armchair,
or a comfortable bed.

I hadn't fought with my sister
though she had provoked me
in all her usual ways.
If I had, Grannie could have told me,
"We women must stick together for
all we have is each other,
we can't depend on the men".

"I spat in their Holy water, Grannie,
I did it for a dare".
The combs teeth bit as the rhythm broke".
"Now there", said Grannie, "is a sin".
The comb started up again
and with it so did Grannie.
"Half the Catholics in the world", she said,
"Are women. It was very wrong to spit.
They could catch anything,
what with the men using it as well".

Grown Up

The crimson blush of lost girlhood
spread itself on the sheet of her shame.
What had she done, Mother, Sister?
I bleed! Have I wounded myself?
Mother, Sister, both tell her
she has done nothing – except
become a woman and
it really doesn't hurt.
Later they threw in the towel
along with the safety pins.

The darkness of the glass of growing
pierced holes in the walls of the womb.
Frightening beauty born of itself,
insomniac days fill themselves
with searches for bridges
across waking and sleeping.
Nights filled with dreams
of strong men on wild horses, riding
riding to save her for themselves
who cannot save herself.

Between times and on bridges
she would not sleep again,
no happy ever after.
Beauty had kissed the beast
and thousands of years had created
the awakening.

Nursery Days And Nights

One midsummer night
I dreamed a dream
of childhood,
a dream of my nursery
days and nights

I watched the sun
roll up its sleeves
to the elbows of the evening,
as he set about to leave the sky

The moon, red faced
could hear a dog bark,
imagined again
a cow had jumped.
It was only the stars
winking bloodshot eyes
at the moon's madness.

They did not see,
as I did,
the dish and the spoon
eloping to another world.

Marigold Tiger

Boyhood still had him
by the shirt-tail,
had not pulled up his socks.
One last, new catapult,
half in, half out, of his pocket
was for the tiger
in the jungle.

This time, hot summertime,
the tiger would be there
drinking the sun-gold
from the river.

Belly-low the boy would cross the bridge.
Stones would bounce across the water
and the tiger would be his.

Summer got there before him.
burned the water from the river.
covered the dry pebble bed
with a soft sprinkling of marigolds.

Mistaking their gold for sun
reflection of tiger
the boy took careful
catapult aim, not once
but often.

Beheading twenty marigolds
he was dismayed to see
his golden tiger burst
into a hundred rays
of marigold sunlight.

That Which Was Lost Is Found

She could see through
the clean water
to the clear
see-through plastic
of the snake bangle

that slithered its
way round her wrist
as she snatched
at the spricks
in the cold river.

She twisted too much
in her conceit
as a sprick-catcher
and watched as
the plastic serpent

glimmered its deceitful
way off her wrist
and was lost,
forever it seemed

until this memory
returned it to her.

The Stripper

Four years old she wears only a wig.
She admires herself in a mirror.
Striptease star, she dances a jig
and doesn't consider it infra dig
that she should wear only the periwig;
after all she is not a concurrer
with great granny's notions
of how she should dress, 'if'
didn't even come into it.
And besides, on her head
she wore great granny's wig
so there couldn't be
very much sin to it.

FAMILY

The Ten Shilling Note

Swirly paper-petticoated frock,
stockings of glass in tip toe shoes
with heels of elegant height,
she was ready for the dance,
with only the red on her lips to blot
and the ten shilling note to put in her purse.
Never mind aunt Jinny sat by the fire
spitting out words of holy threat
about dancing and painted faces.

Gripping a scrap of paper between her lips
then tossing it into the coals
she escaped with a goodbye, I'm late,
and thanks to her Dad for the money.
The man at the station was not sympathetic
when she pushed the scrap of paper under his
glass and asked for a ticket to the next town.

Operation Traveller

You and I have travelled
many roads together.
Crossed paths have parted us.
At corners we turned
one to the other, levelled
between us rough and uphill trails.
Revelled in each easy downhill slope.

Now, for a while, you must
go away from me,
follow a path wholly
and only your own.
You, who hate travelling
will make the best of your journey.

With what you take for the journey
remember to pack my love,
wrapped up in parcels of time
well spent,
tied with bonds of children
and friends and home.
May it be a safe journey.

To A Granddaughter On Her Naming Day

Element of earth energy
-a personality seeking its own name-
so say the cards.
Determined, not easily pushed
But lovingly led and of the earth
-so say the stars.
From your stars and your cards
An earth name is in order.
Knowing nothing of these
Your creatively practical parents
Chose a name for you.
You are Aoife.

I watch your earthy energy
heeling and toeing across the floor,
stopping and starting, oohing and ahhing,
moving always towards the perpendicular.
Aoife, a little earth mother
There, thereing each soft and hard toy.
I watch the space shrink
between your head and this table
that chair - as you grow
towards their undersides.
I watch and wonder at your will.
Pick me up, and put me down,
give me this, take that.
Wordless instruction so clearly given.

Your hello smiles of recognition
fill me to my brim
with love and laughter and thanksgiving
for your presence.
Your absence, the time before your presence
is one of the great imponderables
of western philosophical thought.
Photographs, toys, clothes and thoughts
are the memory aids
I will use in the future.
The task for now is
to hold every ongoing moment
of your present.

It is the nature of grandmothers
to fancy themselves as fairy godmothers,
especially on naming days.
Let me pretend I can touch you
with the wand of love
and grant you the wish
of everything good,
that the stars and the cards
of your life are fulfilled.
I wish that you continue determined
while allowing yourself
to be lovingly led
and that your personality
truly finds the name it seeks,
Aoife – of the earth.

A Birthday Wish

Last year friendly dolphins
disported themselves
in celebration of your birthday.
This year the pansy
illustrates the card
I choose for you.

Did you know, when you chose
the pansy as a favourite flower,
it is a name for several species
of violet including
the shrinking sort, perhaps?
The heart's ease, for sure.

Did you know when you loved
its beautiful crimsons
that pansy is a fanciful use
of the French 'pensee' meaning thought,
in turn from the Latin
'pensare' to weigh?

Did you know the flower's
American cousin is called
Johnny-jump-up?
Or that in unkindness
it is sometimes referred to
as love-in-idleness?

By the power of the flower
embodied in this card I give you
I wish you total heart's ease,
though not quite idleness,
as you pensively weigh
your birthday love in the balance

LOVE

Love Talk

Naked to naked body
on a Sunday morning,
coffee finished
papers and books laid aside;
in anticipation she
enjoyed the groin swell,
the flow of love juice,
said nothing.
In a similar state of body
he said
"do you think this is an emblem
of the relational nature of being"?
She said nothing.

Baptism

Doomed by the wine, trapped
by politeness, late for the naming
they hid themselves
in the trees, Adam-and-eve like.
Deep into Paradise Drive they stumbled,
black stars and the moon sky-high.
Next door a dark garden and dancers
chanting a spell believed
without guile.

Tongue licked tongue in a silence
imperfectly broken – odd car, aeroplane,
not the singing.
Finger tip, nipple, lip, groin swell
that swung them both groundward.
Leaves cracked under spine.
Spine held fast to ground.
Ground swelled under sky.
Sky was kind and dark to them
and she was glad she wore young
wrap-around skirts in this
her fifty-ninth year.

They held their own naming ceremony
called the neighbour's garden
The Fruit Patch.

How Does She Say Thank You

She can only be grateful by feeling so.
Her difficulty lies in the way
to show gratitude by 'doing' gratitude.
If she knew of a way that she could,
well then she would.
What is it that stands in the way
of her doing what pleases him?
Why, if she did, would it not be true
to her, not to him?

He tells her his needs,
indeed he shouts;
his silence screams
his needs to her
of her, for her,
and she is stunned, she is
that frozen, that cold bitch
he says she is.
She is a shivering stone,
grey, hard, needing warmth
and a gentle beckoning to come
to a melting lovingness
that owes nothing to gratitude
and everything to space to grow.

Always Into Spring

May we always be in springtime.
bud and sprout
with beginnings,
even ends be our purposes
and means not interfere
with our darkenings,
or light mornings
clouded over
by dark anticipations.

May our flowers be
of the bulb, daffodil and snowdrop,
lightening the moonstruck
boughs of our behaving.

May we spring
to any autumn.
May we leave
in our forgetfulness
any winter snap
to its own wintering.
to its own time enough.
May we always be
in springtime.

Your Dark Core

Nothing like crystal
shines the great black slate.
Vine of the ocean's sediment,
the slate reflects little
of the embers
warming its cool black heart.

Green sea slime
hides the stone's lustre.
A solitary barnacle
clutches the surface.

Safe from the sea
of your drowning,
within the shell of your fear,
you hide your sombre light,
shrouded in moss,
guarded by mollusc.

To reach your dark core,
uncover the black beauty
of your layered centre,
the tug of the tide
is not enough.
It must become a storm.

Earrings For His Girl

Last wild spring
she pierced her ears
in a storm tossed
bluebell wood,
with a darning needle
sucked to sterility,
borrowed from
her brother's friend.
In return for the loan
she lent her body

on the forest floor,
bluebells dying
of ivy.
Lying about her age
neither she nor her baby
would grow older,
only the boy
whose ivy-threaded needle
stitched her a shroud
to wear with
autumn bluebells.

Her red hair
an autumn forest
where the bluebells
In her ears hung

sadly out of season.
Her blue lips,
a frosted glacier,
catching reflections
of the ringing
of the bluebells.

She Thinks Of Love

On a sandy beach she dreams of him
as pebble and sandworm settle
and the moon silvers the grains
after sand and crawfish have gone to sea,
lost in the tender, evening waves.

In the shadow of a breakwater
she stands beside this dream of him
and he says to her,
"Lady in white cotton gloves
what do you think of love?"

She replies, "I do not think much
of love. It strips me
of my lily white gauntlets.
It is only with my bare hands
I find and love the bones of you."

He asks again, "But, woman,
what do you think of love?"
"I think, I think too much of love.
I am more comfortable
when I wear my gloves".

As the dream of him fades
she hears the breath across the shore,
"Lady, lady, love cannot live

wrapped in white cotton,
it must pour through the skin".
She says again and again,
"There is more comfort,
there is more comfort
in white cotton..."

Harvesting

In my flower garden
I planted love's perennial.
I picked the choicest blooms
from your carpet of gold.
I enjoyed their musk
from root to stem.
I carelessly touched
each green leaf
and drowned them
in watered-down tears.

I forgot to listen, love,
to your gardenspeak.
I sucked the green
from my fingers
in ignorance
of love's horticulture.
I mistook your genus.
I reaped no second harvest.
We had sown only
an annual.
And that only half hardy.

Poppy Days

Black dot poppy seed
bursts into flame;
blushes violet and scarlet;
offers tangy orange
petals of fire
for a short time.

Only the white flower
loiters with intent
to mimic sleep.

She keeps your rainbow posie
in see-through cling film,
as a reminder
of your poppy days,
while she watches
and waits for
the bloom
to fade.

Poems Inspired by Anita's Paintings

Pale Man Sits

Pale man sits. Elbow rests on knee.
Body rests on hand. Hand is on ground.
Green fish-woman stands.
Elbow curves to hold fishtail.
Finger points to pale man.
Blue feathers grow into a head cloud.
Pink tree's twiggy fingers hold
A star? A bat? Perhaps a flower?

What it, that is, the tree, means, is
that pale men who sit under pink trees
are likely to be pointed at by green
fishy-tailed women with their heads
in the clouds while a pink tree
opens its arms to batty, flowery, starry
possibilities. What else?

Freud's Delight

Candle and cave, cave and candle,
whichever way we view it
Sigmund said he had a handle
on what it is to screw it.

Eyes and mountain, mountain and eyes,
look down your nose and dream it,
we go ski-joring on the ice.
Snow fun unless you deem it

natural and good, good and natural.
Whatever sort of sprick
Sig used to catch the mackerel with
the candle needs a wick.

Moonwater Scales

Flat dark sea, black and blue, bruised
by a grey moon, itself burdened.
The weight of the sky presses cobalt
on a sliver of horizon
flat dark sea black and blue

Up from curve of reflected caduceus,
not falling, rising – a female Hermes,
far away Neptuna, black mercurial fish
salutes the moon in silhouette,
up from the curve of caduceus.

Balancing forces of moon and water,
a split reflection forms scaly ellipses
of mind and matter, supporting the shadow.
Half fish of Neptune, half woman of Diana,
Balancing forces.

All Trees Are Pink- aren't they?

Forked In a rosy – fIngered tree
a green winged creature waits.
Limpet-like, a blue cat sees
only a bite for its supper plate.

Cat looks at creature with only a glance
blind in the light of the moon,
blue cats, like us, have never a chance,
like us he will ever oppugn.

Pink tree, green sky, the pale lunar light,
fit home for the magical beast.
But for us blue cats if we hunt at night
those colours will serve us least.

Blue cats can whistle up a gale
but only if we choose
will the wind's rough tongue uncurl our tails
and then we contrive to use

the shadows cast by the pink tree's trunk
to leap like a dance. We will
land on our feet as we are wont.
Question is! Will the beast be there still?

Senses

Two leaves adrift in a boat,
nose inhaling.
Eyes cannot see as leaves float,
sailing towards the mouth.
Will it taste leafy strangeness?

When the ear does not hear,
and the eye does not see,
the nose is all knowing.
It knows the leafy boat
sails towards the indigo dark
from its dish of achromatic grey.

At first I want to paint the leaves
with remembered yellow of buttercups,
transform them into candle flame.
I would move my sun-filled bowl
under the chin of the nose,
just checking if butter is adored.

The Kiss

Out of the mouth? – Or
into whatever, the dove,
bird of love and promise
to carry her from sky
to ultramarine floor
on the gold of a kiss.
Missing the pluck of beak

is the bird taking
from those blue lips-or
giving? Who is the feeder,
who the fed? – up
blue air, deep down navy sea,
down below, the feathers
fluffing lines of promise.

Stare at eye, air. See
feathers fall as beak
pierces lip and tongue.
Speak, love –
no more kissing.

Letting Go

A blue rabbit crosses
my green path.
Is he flying?
Or is it that I am
sunk in the blue, green
sand of a black shore?
Blues of many seas
wave behind me.
Where has the sky gone?

My green leaves flower
into the sky, red, orange, white.
My mask is in place
but I forgot my snorkel.
When I am under water
I shall drown
before my violet eyes
can see what lies below

Red passion broken free-
the orange flame of
energy is let loose.
Only the white purity
clings to its stalk,
leaf-sheltered and safe
to make its descent
to the black depths
of letting go.

Attraction of Opposites

Tenderly touching a smooth white breast
a green spiky creature hovers,
sees softly, perfectly eye-to-eye
with a delicately winged lover.

Together they stand in a forest grove
of cobalt earth and indigo sky.
Strange to us, who are not of their world
all we can do is wonder why.

All we can see, perhaps, is the wood,
the flowers and butterflies murmuring low
among tall trunks of leafless trees
where in darkness we would not go.

We ask ourselves, then, "are things as they
seem?
Can a green and prickly beast
be joined to the smooth and the white?"
We answer, "not in the least."

But then we remember fat Mr. Jones
with his ginger hair and his bald patch,
lover of Jennifer, skinny and blond,
yet everyone called it a love match.

As well we remember short Billy Bones,
toothless and silent; grim and morose.

His lover was Lulubelle, tall as a pole,
no missing teeth but a tongue quite verbose.

In the dark forest the world as they know it
the green and the white creatures smile.
Green face to white face tenderly touch.
They know lovers find their right space.

People and Predicaments

Encounter Group

There was an encounter
with moon over water.
A silver thread completes
a moon-silvered crescent.
Presents, she was told,
she had a flair for.
Her head responded.
"Do I have", it asked,
"a flair for absence?"

In that moment
the absence was only for him,
the answer fraught with difficulty.
Now, at this time,
for all of them, the absence
of them she knew would come.

Drawn by that silver thread,
dread of the onslaught
of the absence, grew into
present apprehension
and the net was there.

Names and addresses and
telephone numbers,
reassuring Moroccan stones
to be dropped into

the pool of the moon,
cupped safely in the crescent
held by the handle
of the silver thread.

Life Stories

Lovers in tall houses
need strong limbs
to head for heights,
descend cellar depths.
But once enter a room
at any level
and free fall may occur.
In cellar darkness
mushroomed memories
hide their poison
among cobwebbed secrets;
old rocking chairs, broken promises;
and the wine bottles
of past and future
celebrations.

Through the door, first floor
lovers are grounded.
Sit, dine, withdraw,
hold conversations;
putting their house in order
to put it on the market,
or to throw stones.
They forget the advice given
to people who live
in glass houses.

On occasion in bedrooms
ecstasy beyond the call of duty
takes faithful lovers by surprise,
helps them forget other moments
in other houses
where bedrooms were out of bounds
and visiting lovers
were expected
to behave politely.

Under the dormers,
hothead of the house
creativity of different kinds
is let loose to swoon
on restless summer nights.

Reading, painting, writing these lines-
considering the height of the roof
a night on the tiles
offers wild possibilities.

Women at an Auction

Four women stood under the hammer.
Four masters of the craft, from common clay
had shaped their own ideas of woman;
one fat black-robed Persian girl,
alongside a slender twenties flapper,
a rough-hewn Polly with her kettle
and beside her - ubiquitous Madonna.

The hammer fell to the Highest Bidder.
'Sold to you, Madam. In the sky blue suit'
On to the next lot, which nobody looked at.
The attention of the crowd was occupied
watching the woman in the blue suit
wrest the hammer from the auctioneer.

The crowd's loud intake of breath
was lost in the sound of the hammer
as it came down four times over.
The Highest Bidder's words fell
into the silence that cleared the air,
'I'm glad to have shattered
these illusions, now I'll pay'
The auctioneer said,
'Indeed you will, woman.
Indeed you will.'

Nursery Myths

You little Jack Horner! You there!
Which good little boy are you?
Who is this plum you have pulled?
Out of which pie has she come?
Don't be fooled, be Nimble Jack,
for she is not the sugar-n-spice
cookie she seems.
Nor is she your 'and Jill'
whipped into shape by a silly
Goose Mother knowing no better.
She lays golden eggs, very nice
but not as Georgie Porgie's prize
when he made her so ridiculed.

Contrary Mary has nothing on her,
and that doesn't mean what it might.
The garden's just fine.
She protects it from blight,
from the slugs, and the snails
and those puppy dogs' tails,
as well as from persons who might,
as blue-suited spiders
sit close beside her
to blow their horn
amongst the corn
and lead her up a garden path
into a parlour or on to a hearth –
now that's not cricket!

On Not Moving House

I am angry
about the cherry tree
left so long waiting
in black plastic.

I prepared
a movable space for it,
vast clay pot, not
too heavy for men to lift.

The tree will die of waiting
for a smooth patio slab
where its pot might balance
the earthy roots.

Contained in my own
black-bagged anger
I want to plant myself
in a greater space of possibility
where my attic collections
of boxes and books and magic theatres
will not die for lack of space.

I wait and watch
over the cherry tree.
I think of my high hopes
waiting their turn
packed tight under the roof slope
of my unmoved house.

Hanging Baskets

Last year the flower baskets splashed
summer colour on the wall..
Winter wiped away shades and scents.
The snails appeared as
the rain, falling and falling,
turned the wall to ash grey.
She allowed the snails to live there
in their shell houses, whose earth colour
blended ill with the wall's winter wash.
She did not welcome the snails,
but could only evict them
by smashing their fragile houses.
Instead she extended their leasehold
and watched the decay
of hanging foliage.

This year a families of birds set up house
in the neglected flower baskets.
The arrival of these residents
created all the necessary fuss
of occupying a new house.
The neighbours ignored each other
until the children arrived
and the food supply became important.
The birds turned on the snails,
smashed them from their shells
with their sweet cruel beaks.

Next year she will hang her flowers
in the earth where they belong,
give the wall, unpainted, to the snails
and plant a tree in her garden
for the birds.

The Pearl Of Great Price

My oyster shell is no shield
against a small sand flaw
washed inshore to beach there.
At first given to small waves of anger,
later to spumed roars
of great sea horses
dashing at my head.
In time, a sea of experience
washes the soft lining of the shell,
around a sand speck,
till it wears a lustrous coat.

Only when the oyster knows
the irritation of the grit,
soothed with the help
of the pure salt waters;
only when the pearl
is prised from the depths
of the sea and the shell;
only then can my private rage
be worn as public virtue.

Against the warm skins
of friends and lovers
my angry pearls
improve their lustre.

Cats Eye View

We built the greenhouse
right in the middle
of the field.
God knows why.
I took my cat
into the greenhouse
and explained to her
(the cat not God)
that this was not
a place she should be.
This would in fact
be her only visit.
She (the cat not God)
listened patiently
as cats do.

Just then someone
appeared in a parka,
very large boots
and carrying a great spade.
To me he looked apocalyptic,
to the cat - who knows?
(God, not the cat?)
She (the cat not God)
took fright. I had closed
the greenhouse door
meaning to get her

(the cat not God)
used to the habit.

The cat raced around
the greenhouse walls
and smashed her way
out head first.
She shot across the field,
disappearing into a ditch.
I thought surely
she had been decapitated.

But when I found her
(the cat not God)
there she was
sitting quietly
with that look in her eye.

The Old Woman

The Old Woman Sets Out

Once upon many a time
a long-toothed woman set out
on a journey to a place.
She took with her a back- pack
to put things behind her
and so in perspective
she said, so to speak.

Into the back-pack she put
a history book and a mask
to wear before strangers,
a bright red lipstick she never wore
on account of her long tooth,
a small fat cat to get thin,
and for use as a dream pillow.

She also took a few words
in case of emergencies.
Along the way she used the book
to remind her of where she had come from,
especially on those occasions
when she failed to unpack the mask
on encountering strangers.

When words, or the cat,
refused to be let out of the bag,
it was then the emergency words

came into their own
and talked about the weather,
health, children, futures and,
sometimes, pasts.

There were naturally things
in the bag that she would
prefer, at nearly all times,
not to bring out-or think out.
Words not meant for emergencies
she kept to herself.
We shall see perhaps,
sometime, what these are.
She shared them with the cat,
who listened, as cats will.

The Old Woman's Nightmare

Once upon a night
then, not now,
for cat is very thin,
the old woman,
head rising and rising,
on the soft fur
belly breath of her
dream pillow cat,
dreamed a dream...

in each of her long-fingered palms
she held tight to a stone.
From her left hand exotic peacock
feathers sprouted into gigantic wings
and the great stone flew
from her fingers, hovering;
a wicked beak pushed out
of the gentle stone in her right,
penetrated the soft skin
and it sprang a bloody cataract
from the pointing finger.

No sign where
the peacock might fly to
nor why the stone pierced where it did.
Instead, without notice, she was
in a melange of soldiers,

cowering, not wanting conflict.
A tiny man came at her.
He is her torturer.
On his hands bladed gloves
to scrape car windscreens
or the skin off rabbits.

He advances and suddenly
she knows she can stop him
by thumbing his skinny old armpits
akimbo – the torturer turns
to a scarecrow, black feathers,
no peacock. Cat pillow stirs.
Cat has her own dreams,
as the old woman's dream fades.

Old Woman Reads The Book

One day when there was none to look,
the old woman sat on a roadside rock.
With grit she took up the book of myths.
It fell open – dark pits before her – at a page
far back in history, a stage in her trail,
blazed by the adults of her adolescence.

Like jacks-in-the-box the words jumped up,
"Don't ever tell. Don't ever! Never tell" and
"If you love me…!" She never did.
The book gazumped the memory, letters
refused their mandate, unfettered truths
she had scarcely begun to wonder through.

Questions were asked in the house
of her girlhood. Rules made not to break.
The 'shall nots' were question and answer,
blocking everything the 'shalts' allowed,
The final score was hardly a draw,
'Yes' to everyone, 'no' to her.

Looking In and Looking Out

Changing The Rules

OK, here are the rules.

Record

the emotion and mind
you are objective.

Remember

life situations are
distinctive to each
individual telling.
You are always
that individual.

Trust

your own telling.

Start

anywhere and go on
to somewhere.

Dream

plenty and dream some more.

Recall

the amazingness
of what we wear.

Remember

the purple and scarlet
skirts and shawls,
the black lace stockings
they said you wouldn't dare;

Remember, too,

the very shocking pink
silk slip – not the sort
with built-up shoulders,
but the tenderest of
slender shoelace straps.

Don't forget

the cool kimono,
snarling with dragons
whose red hot tongues
licked your eighteen inches
of unstayed waist.

and remember,

the slick
shine of your black patent
six inch stilettos - and...

Remember

to tiptoe.

On Being Self-Composed

If you want to sing a song of yourself
it is not enough to hum the tune.
You must know the words, all of them,
no matter how hard to learn and remember.
Keep repeating the lines, inventing new ones
as you go along. Even the tune can change.
But don't ever go flat or sharp.
Keep singing in the key you've chosen, for now.
You can always use bar rests
to catch your breath and swallow your spit.
Now and then you might try a duet.
But be warned of the risk of disharmony
and the possibility that the other voice
will be singing an entirely different song.

buttercups and daisies

(a tribute to e.e.cummings)

the daisy
looked dog-tired and blue
and gave me no answer
when i stripped its petals
one by one so
now i do not know
if you will be there to ask
the buttercup
about my fat wishes

Second Death

Last petal, pale as a shroud
fringed with rust,
dropped from the rose
and fell to its death;
came to rest for a moment
on the table top
till someone opened the door
and the draught carried
the petal away.

Having cut down the flower
she always kept it
too long in a vase.

Out Of The Dark And Into The Light - A Dream

Imagine a landscape framed in a circle.
A chicken with a bright golden egg light
at the centre of its breast,
surrounded by black feathers,
its beak-to-spine a shining plait.
See its long shadowed legs.
The legs are running fast across the circle.
Notice the chicken is not headless,
a fine yellow wig trailing in the air.
Follow the direction of its running.
Behind, black shadow ghosts,
their arms outstretched fiercely reaching,
trying to pull the chicken back to the shadows.
Look ahead of the running and see, mirrored,
yellow shadow-ghosts,
arms gently seeking, calling the chicken
to the golden light on their side of the circle.
This chick is perhaps a roadrunner
but she doesn't know
she carries the light with her
to the egg at her centre.

Picture That

The day I called at the gallery,
two paintings,
white sea, dark sea,
colour and shadow.
A picture thinly painted.

Monastic site
in County Louth,
overlooking the Boyne Valley.

The green grassy slopes
of the middle ground
had depth, the yellow
thickness of intention.

The brassy orange of burnt
foreground was faded away
to fawn. Retreated
from viewers' eyes,

gave way to the vicious emerald
with barely a quorum
of orange flashes
to make their point,
earthed in the green grass.

Instead – a retrogressive march

of pale mud- coloured mounds
finally lost perspective,
and on to the...
next painting please.

Moonwalker

She who carries the moon
and the stars in her arms
carries too the knowing of them.
What and how she knows
she will sometimes tell
to one who truly wishes
to know and use the telling
for those they will gift
with the moon and stars.

She has lost the moon.
It is more a clouding
over, a misunderstanding,
a whim which might bear starfruit.
Watch, you will see the star
shine in her belly,
blossom on her skin
till it bursts to unsheathe
the precious bud,
or spill its monstrous blood.

It was the stars in her eyes
which began the ebb and flow
of the passion which made her
forget the moon's treason.
That cloud of romantic trust
covered both moon and stars,

hid all but passion and lust.
Sensation soon to come.

The Anarchist

Go suck
the finger puppet.
Thumb your nose
at strings pulled
by jackasses
heehawing in passages
of power.
Your own finger tip
control is in order.

Add your touch.
Count to a million-
one by one-
if you want to.
Trust your own telling
and start somewhere,
anywhere
you're at just now.

Dream words
if you have to;
do anything but sleep.
and remember.
You are the dictator.
Make the words,
leap to the page.
Write your own
POEM!

For Fun

Blooming Wild

What if
snowdrops fell
and bluebells rang
and honey suckled?

What if
the primrose blushed
and meadows rued
the horsing around
of the old chestnuts?

What if
dandy lions
roared all day,
would they become
 the leopard's bane,
or get up the nose
of the wild sneezewort?

Well!

Even if the willow wept
or Virginia crept about
and witch Hazel
wreaked loose strife.
I'd still be the hero
of this plot

if Rosemary
forget me-not.

Lightning Source UK Ltd.
Milton Keynes UK
UKHW021252240121
377545UK00006B/32